FAST MUSIC

HUGO WILLIAMS

Fast Music

faber

First published in 2024
by Faber & Faber Ltd
The Bindery, 51 Hatton Garden
London EC1N 8HN

Typeset by Faber & Faber Ltd
Printed in the UK by TJ Books Ltd, Padstow, Cornwall

A CIP record for this book is available from the British Library

ISBN 978–0–571–38261–3

2 4 6 8 10 9 7 5 3 1

Acknowledgements

To the editors of *London Magazine*, *London Review of Books*, *New Statesman*, *The Spectator* and *Times Literary Supplement*. Some of the poems first appeared in two pamphlets: *Badlands* (Mariscat Press) and *The West Pier* (New Walk). I would like to thank Jane Feaver and Matthew Hollis for their help.

to Maren Meinhardt

Contents

11

I

Undiscovered Islands

On a dusty desk, in the east wing
of my castle, sits my typewriter
and my typewriter sits on my desk
every day and night, never says a word.

    – MICKEY JUPP, song lyric

Days going down with a splash and a hiss
into a restless sea,
words returning with a bang and a bell
to the left-hand margin,
pausing for a moment to reflect on the scene.

Nights struggling with the syntax of storms,
the grammar of dreams,
words setting out in lifeboats
in search of lost meanings,
tossing and turning in their sleep.

Words in mortal combat
with arm-wrestling octopi and squid.
Cries rising from near extinction
in luminous bubbles,
days going down with the ship.

Sun lifting its tousled head
out of yesterday's wreckage
washed up on the shore,
words bearing news of undiscovered islands,
sometimes taking us there.

Pennies from Heaven

Spots of Leichner '5' and '9'
alternate round my father's face like warpaint
in his dressing-room mirror.
He rubs them down to a healthy tan
for the part of Julian
in 'We at the Crossroads' at Her Majesty's.
Next morning, dressed to kill
in government-issue busman's overcoat,
long in the sleeve
(white armband for 'Officer Material'),
he finds himself drilling
with other actor-volunteers
in the Queen's Westminsters,
presenting tightly furled umbrellas
in the pouring rain.

'Don't just do something, sit there'
is the word of command
to the men guarding Staines Railway Bridge
during the Phoney War.
My father, whose debts to the Inland Revenue
amount to four figures,
receives only eight shillings and sixpence
in his weekly wage packet,
about what it cost him
to look after his top hat before the war.
He has placed the coins on the railway line
and let a train pass over them.
Now they are larger, flatter,
and completely useless,
except as playthings for his son.

Fast Music

The faster the better perhaps,
but not always for the best.
When 'Tico Tico' came on the radio in 1944
I ran round the room on the furniture,
I took off in a Spitfire.
The music stopped suddenly
and I crashed to earth,
shot down by an invisible enemy.
I must have tripped on the wire.
I was trying to push it back
when a flash of electricity
soldered my fingers together.
My tipsy grandmother
was babysitting asleep upstairs.

I came home from hospital
wearing a solid glove
made of plaster-of-paris,
inscribed 'to a soldier in the wars'.
A wind-up gramophone
was waiting in my room
playing 'Tico Tico' by Ethel Smith.
I wanted to dance on the turntable,
the faster the better.
I was never so happy
as when my grandmother wound me up
and bounced me over the moon
on a lap of honour.
Black bakelite planets spun me to heaven.

Somewhere Else

I found myself somewhere else,
up north and over to the left.
I was given a new name
and told to sit still.
All my things were on a shelf,
including my cars.
If one of the screws came loose
everything fell on the floor.

I was so far away from home
I hardly existed.
I was a distant memory,
a little old man of seven,
forgetful and quiet.
I sat with my back to the wall.
'Is your mother a prostitute, Williams?'
I said I didn't know.

I taught myself to write in about a week,
remembering things
and hiding them with my arm.
'How is my bike? How is Sam?
Don't let Sam ride my bike.'
My handwriting unwound
like the slow-moving wire
of the fire escape mechanism,

screaming for help
as it lowered me to the ground
on Fire Practice Day.
Everyone was shouting my name,
telling me where to put my feet
when I got stuck in the ivy.
A photo of me crying
appeared in the school magazine.

The Moths

'Don't worry, darling, three months
will soon fly past, you'll see.
Then you'll be coming home again
to your own little room upstairs.'

Every night I watched
the poor blind things flying past,
burning their papery wings
on the strip lighting of the dormitory.

Fear School

Stewart is 'Suet'. On a whim
a Mr Park takes hold of him.

He asks the question 'Why so fat?'
And what can Suet say to that?

O foolish Suet, slow to see,
that Mr Park is fat as thee!

But Mr Park says Suet's slack
and sends him round the football track.

'And Suet, baby, just for fun,
take your belongings on your run.'

Now Suet crawls to Mr Park,
dragging a vengeance through the dark.

I Don't Know, Sir

When they catch us red-handed,
flicking ink pellets in class,
passing notes behind their backs,
they always ask the same question:
what do we think we're doing
and who is responsible for this mess?
When they take us by the ear
and ask who we think we are
and when are we going to grow up,
we can only think of one answer.

When they ask us privately, man to man,
how we plan to earn a living
if we never listen in class,
we find ourselves searching the horizon
for a life in the real world
and have to admit we don't know.
When they catch us out of bounds,
and ask where we think we're going,
smoking and wearing the wrong shoes,
we answer truthfully enough.

My Future

When I was caught writing poetry
under the desk in History
I was sent to see the Chaplain
to have a chat about my future.

I imagined a confessional scene
with a pep-talk and a penance,
but the Chaplain only asked me
if I'd been feeling depressed lately.

Did I have a friend I could talk to
about my problem? I said yes,
I had two friends, but they weren't
interested in poetry. Nobody was.

The Chaplain smiled to himself
and said he had several poet-friends.
He wrote poetry himself actually.
There was nothing to be ashamed of.

'Louise my niece is a fine poet.
Autumn Journal is my favourite.
I'd be happy to show it to you.
I could introduce you if you like.'

I pictured a beautiful pious girl
with long blond hair and blue eyes
and said I wouldn't mind.
I seemed to have got off lightly.

i.m. Tara Browne (1945–1966)

I read the news today, oh boy,
about a lucky man who made the grade.
  – THE BEATLES, 'A Day in the Life'

London had barely started
when you blew into town
with your charmed existence,
your cursed Lotus Elan.
You asked me once if I wanted to drive
and we changed places for a moment.
'Come on, Hugo, put your foot down!'
I touched the accelerator
and the thing took off like a bird
down the King's Road.
I don't know where we were going
because I got out and walked.

You entered the 1964
Mercantile Credit Trophy, Formula Three,
but officials found fault
with your windscreen,
which wasn't laminated.
You knocked it through with your elbow
and turned your jacket back to front
to counter the wind factor.
You won by three seconds,
'the sensation of the meeting' (Autosport).
It was the first lap
of your race to oblivion.

For a couple of multi-coloured years,
while *Help!* gave way to *Revolver*,
life got in the way.
With identical blond pageboys
and Cheshire cat grins
you and your friend Brian Jones
sat up all night
like ghosts of yourselves,
playing with your train set
and tripping to heaven
while King's Road toadies
draped themselves round the walls.

From *Out of Our Heads* to *Aftermath*,
you parked your pretty car
outside the Scotch or Ad Lib club,
while the world dished out its favours
to a lucky few
who could dance all night
and sleep it off next day.
You danced on the accelerator.
You didn't notice that the lights had changed,
but spun the car around
to protect your girlfriend
and went to face the music on your own.

Death Letter

after Tristan Corbière

You trusted me with the boy
and now he's gone. What can I say?
That it won't happen again?
That I'll make it up to you?
I'd have given my right arm
to send him home to you in one piece,
but someone up there
must have taken a liking
to the boy with sticking-out ears.
Now he's teaching the angels
how to dance the Charleston,
kicking up his heels
on a minefield in heaven.

God knows, it's a hard apprenticeship,
dying for your country
in this tropical paradise,
dancing for a dinner of hot lead.
Our boy must have ordered a drum-roll
of machine-gun fire
before taking his last bow.
We're all of us dying like flies
on this holiday of a lifetime.
The graveyard is fully booked!
It won't be long
till I'm tripping the light myself
on a dance floor in heaven.

Pause for Thought

My eyes are cast down,
as if from modesty or embarrassment.
My half-closed hands
lie on the table in front of me
where I can see them.

From the way I am sitting,
staring at a sheet of paper,
something would seem to be the matter.
Perhaps I am ill?
Or the temperature of my pen won't come down?

I lean over myself
with a concerned expression on my face,
as if I am visiting.
I think of something kind to say.
My pen moves over the paper for a moment

like the needle of an instrument
for recording brain-life.
From the other side of the street
I look like someone writing.
My head comes up, as if I am pausing to think.

Nowhere Man

Remind me to look up one or two
old girlfriends to isolate socially with
in these jolly times. Only joking.
I'm so sick and tired
of my own endangered company
that I'm seriously considering
chucking up everything and just clearing off,
like that chap in Larkin.
I too detest my room with its good books,
its specially chosen junk.
I'd willingly swagger the nut-strewn roads
stubbly with goodness
if it meant escaping this peculiar
ruined afterlife we seem to have invented,
but where else is there to go?

Shirt Story

Everything looked so promising
when I went round with some wine
to try on the shirt she'd made me
on her new machine.

There it lay on the bedside table
in the light of the dimmer switch,
an old piece of flowery material
transformed by her loving stitch.

We would drink to the happy occasion
as I tried on the waiting gift,
but the wine tasted sour to the drinkers
and the evening started to abort
when the collar stuck out sideways
and the sleeves were far too short.

Lapse

However much more polite
it would have been
to leave her body at home
when she went out

she was obliged to take it with her
everywhere she went
and people in the street
couldn't help noticing this.

Artist and Model

When two heads came together
that should have stayed apart
and two birds of a feather
were shot down by love's dart
the picture seemed to falter
in the looking-glass of art.

There was something left unpainted
or something left unsaid
that showed a perfect stranger
in the light the candle shed
that used to look so like her
until they went to bed.

Heartbreakfast

I seem to have broken my heart.
I was carrying it upstairs on a tray
like a piece of conceptual art,
when I slipped and broke my heart.
You were playing the critical part.
I knew what you would say:
'If you don't want to break your heart,
don't bring it to me on a tray.'

Bad Sex

Even though she was thirty years my junior
and related to me by marriage
I couldn't help feeling put out
when she announced her engagement
to a young novelist of our acquaintance.
What they'd really like as a wedding gift
would be one of my super columns
for the *TLS*, something light but serious,
that could be used on the cover of his
ground-breaking auto-fiction, *Bad Sex*.
She could let me have one or two
amusing anecdotes about his private life
that would bring out his humorous side.
After all, it wouldn't cost me anything.

A Brief Exchange

The self-appointed guardian of our street
stands all day in the doorway
of the house opposite,
glaring at everyone who passes.

His job is making sure the sun never shines
on his side of Raleigh Street.
He holds out his hand for rain
and storm clouds gather to his cause.

I spoke to him once
about some misdirected mail I'd received,
saying my own mail sometimes went astray
to nearby Raleigh Mews.

Did he know that Sir Walter
had a concession on alehouses in the area?
I found myself rambling on
about my long-time hero, explaining

how one of the original fireplaces
of the Old Queen's Head in Essex Road
survives in the present-day pub.
I liked to imagine the poet

leaning there, smoking a pipe of Virginia.
There was surely no truth in the legend
that someone threw a pint over him,
thinking he was on fire?

Not a flicker from the bad weather man.
He held out his hand for rain
and a few indifferent drops
showed their contempt for my blow-in.

'It used to be called St Thomas Street
before the war,' he snarled.
'You can still see the old name
painted on the brickwork over there.'

The Partition

Another gulp of cold coffee
and still nothing going on creatively
when her voice comes sweetly commanding
from behind the partition:
'Have you got any ink?'
I assume she means for the printer,
so I take it through to her.
'No, no, not that sort of ink. Ink ink.'

I find an old bottle of Quink
and return to my cold coffee,
where nothing is still progressing as before.
I'm waiting anxiously
for her next communication
when she comes in smiling triumphantly,
saying she's found a hole in my jacket,
do I want it mending?

A Brilliant Trick

Being well is such a brilliant trick
with all its happy healthy fun.
Nobody likes you when you're sick.

They think you're being melodramatic
trying to divert attention
from their own habitual trick

of appearing busy and energetic
all the time, so that no one
suspects them of being sick.

They can't imagine your chronic
ill health and depression
are anything more than a cheap trick

to make people more sympathetic
to your phoney mental condition
with its outward air of being sick.

All you can do is try to mimic
the way healthy people carry on.
Being well is a useful trick.
Everyone hates you when you're sick.

Enter Mr White

'It's the white man,'
announces Nurse Anthony,
wheeling what looks like
a corpse into the ward.
Swing doors bang shut behind them.

Sentenced to daily piercings
on a lie detector-cum-confessional,
Mr White is held in place
by an exoskeleton of tubes,
pumps and stainless steel rods.

He may be alive or he may be dead,
it hasn't been decided yet.
'If it's got a pulse, we dialyse,'
explains Nurse Anthony,
pushing a stare-eyed Mr White

down a line of hospital beds
like the tortured waxwork of a saint
being trundled through the streets
of a Mexican village
on the Day of the Dead.

Hospital Pet

An invisible pet inhabits my left arm.
It talks to me all day long
in a soft vibrating monotone called a 'thrill'.
It buzzes impatiently,
as if to summon my assistance.
I lay my hand on its head to stop it worrying.
I wrap it in a cold cloth.

My pet is prone to heart attacks called 'blows',
which are not good news.
When one of these occurs
we have to go to A&E for a fistulaplasty.
We sit together in the waiting room,
rocking back and forth in one another's arms,
holding each other's hand.

Probably Poor Later

No more getting better.
No more waking up one morning
feeling like your old self again.
Let's call what's-her-name,
see what's going on.
None of that any more.
No more hitting the street
with a spring in your step
and your knee all right.
Don't even think about it.

You'd like to go out of course,
to see if you still exist,
but you can't obey yourself now,
it hurts too much.
You sit in your chair all day
turning a funny colour.
Where's that list you made?
Someone takes you by the arm
and says how well you're looking.
You haven't changed a bit!

Patient

after Mallarmé

My hair is no bunch of lilies
stuck in a funeral urn
for the approval of the angels.

It laps my body in hot smells,
as if some animal breathed on me.
It mocks my garment's stale chastity.

I lie here stiff with horror at its caresses,
until I am half in love
with the shock my hair inspires.

It thrills and frightens me.
It makes me whole. I'll live forever
in the listless wreckage of my innocence.

I'll stand alone on this monotonous earth
and feel on my useless flesh
the sunset's clammy touch.

Wrapped in my scented shroud,
I'll crouch like a reptile on my parchment bed,
swaying my neck to and fro,

while in the glass my hair's metallic sheen
hoards my nakedness from the world
and wild beasts howl . . .

i.m. The West Pier (1866–2003)

Piers are stepping-stones
out of this world, a line of poetry
flung out to sea on a whim,
a dazzle of sea lights
glimpsed between floorboards.

For 50p you can study eternity
through a telescope
and never have to go there,
only promenade to nowhere and back
in an atmosphere of ice cream.

We used to take the speedboat ride
between the two piers,
pulling the canvas up to our chins
when the spray flew in our faces.
Now we stand and stare

at the remains of our innocence,
twisted girders piled up
in a heap of dead holidays,
while Brighton limps out to sea
on its one good leg.

*

There it is over there,
a little rusty island moored offshore,
the empty cage of its dome
lying lower in the water
every time I come down.
Where are the luminous dolphins
on the merry-go-round?
Buffalo Bill's Wild West?

They could have saved the old pier,
but they gave it away to the crabs
and put up a giant pogo-stick
on the seafront,
a middle finger to its memory.
Now only seagulls cry
in what's left of the concert hall,
only storms shift the scenery.

It sinks below the horizon,
a black and tangled sunset
surrounded by bubbles.
Madame Esmeralda, gypsy fortune-teller,
presses her lips to the glass
of her waterlogged cubicle
and gurgles her apologies
for getting it all so wrong.

Leaving Faces

They turn to look back at me
like riders on a golden galloper,
their smiles in half-profile.

They were going places once,
setting off into the blue
without a care in the world,

but they never arrived there,
only hovered in mid-air,
their smiles losing definition.

With what bright eyes
I studied those leaving faces,
now blasted and frail.

With what shocked innocence
I watch them swaying to and fro
on the gibbet memory.

Their lives are shorter now,
their laughter lost
in the clatter of things falling.

Leaving faces never left home,
they hung about upstairs,
watching time fly

to the sound of fairground music.
No longer dangerous or young,
they are strangely genial,

glazed in other-worldliness,
like hunting trophies of themselves,
shrunken heads on sticks.

I bump into one of them occasionally
with a drink in my hand
and mutter an apology.

Flâneur

Something of the faded dandy
hangs about God's moth-eaten evening coat,
his worn-out cloth-uppers.
He seems to be cruising lost time
in search of fellow flâneurs
who might remember him
from the good old days
before he dyed his hair. He holds out
a threadbare mauve suede glove
as if begging forgiveness
from the crowds of memories
pushing past him in the street.

Thinking I've seen him before somewhere
and feeling vaguely ashamed
of the white silk handkerchief
overflowing the pocket of my suit,
I slip him a few quid
to buy himself a coffee and croissant.
A sudden violent shudder
passes through God's frail form
as he turns himself into
a flowering magnolia tree,
its creamy white petals bending low
in seasonal farewell.

II

The Plunge Club

As if anything needed adding
to the flyer of seven naked girls
getting ready to dive from a high bridge
(*Art Lovers Everywhere*
are Invited to Immerse Themselves Wholly
in Wilful Live Art
at London's Premiere Performance Playground)
she has scribbled a few words of her own:
'If you've got nothing better to do
next Thursday, why not hold your nose
and join us in watery celebration
of anything you like
at the Plunge Club on Lisburn Avenue.
You *can* swim can't you?'

Badlands

For a second I glimpse her animal self
rounding up wild horses
in the book I'm reading
on my way to the club:
Rendez-vous in El Paso,
A Tale of the Old West.
Her feeling for the work doesn't surprise me.
She's probably rounding up
one or two maverick stallions as I speak.
I'm hot on her trail,
riding the rails across town,
from Angel to Kensal Green,
refusing to look up from my book
till I enter the Badlands myself.

Disco Love

When they get to their feet to dance
they know in their hearts
they are dancing with nothing on.
For here are nocturnal creatures,
strangers to one another and themselves,
twisting and turning together
in figures of feigned indifference,
changing partners on a whim.
They might be tightrope walkers,
mating in public on a spotlight's beam,
coupling and uncoupling in mid-air
in their brief attempt at flight,
defying gravity and depravity
for the duration of their love.

Them

They must be messengers from God,
reminding us why we are here.
They process ahead of us like saints,
leading the way to heaven.
We follow them on our knees
into the confessional.
We would follow them to the ends of the earth
just to die in their arms.
If one of them was willing
to sleep with us in our dreams
and was still there next morning,
everything would be strangely peaceful
in our lives and I for one
would be rich and famous by now.

Whatever Love Is

I don't care who I make love with
so long as it is love we make,
which it always is
when I don't know who you are,
when you don't know who I am.
I don't care what we do
so long as we stick our tongues
down one another's throat
and utter incomprehensible cries,
so long as it is love we make
and not some kindly kissing,
which it never will be
if you don't know who you are,
if I don't know who I am.

Bite-marks

Are women naked, do you think,
or is it impossible to say
when they turn around
and walk ahead of you up the stairs?
Looking doesn't help.
Looks leave only bite-marks
down the backs of knees,
or somewhere thereabouts.
Words can't make sense of it.
You find yourself talking in moans
which don't translate very well.
Your mouth fills up with spit
as you try to explain. You're too excited
and dumb to even swallow it.

Visiting Late

Visiting late, I don't put on the light.
I undress in the dark,
throw my things on a chair.
I feel my way towards the bed,
where she is lying quite still,
breathing naturally,
knowing who it is,
but pretending to be asleep.
I think she likes being terrified
by someone she doesn't know
doing something she doesn't expect –
untucking the bottom of the bed,
crawling in like a crocodile,
biting the inside of her leg.

Sell-by Date

Remember johnnies? Slippery fuckers
that seemed like a good idea at the time,
but always spoiled things later?
You kept one in your wallet for years,
until it disintegrated from neglect.
You could feel the little rubbery circle
sliding around in its laminate square,
reminding you of something, but what?
That was about as near as you got
to the real thing, before its longed-for
lubricity reached its sell-by date.
You could be reasonably sure
your wallet wouldn't be opening
before that, never mind her bedside drawer.

Bed of Ashes

As if taking hold
of a long-handled coal shovel
and scraping the remains
of the day's smouldering clinkers
from their bed of ashes
still shimmering and simmering
on the floor of a little stove
and hurling them as hard
and as far as possible
with such perfect satisfaction
and a welcome slow agony
into the great unknown –
a sudden glittering diamond shower
of a snuffed and dying star.

The Happier Life

London was a map of the world
stretched between us.
We stepped off into the blue
in search of the happier life.
We had travelled barely an inch
into the great unknown,
when we lost our way to heaven.
The map turned out to be
no more than a coloured curtain
drawn between us.
We balanced on its edges,
waving to one another across town,
coming close for a moment,
slipping down into its folds.

You Can Tell

You can tell from the way they inhabit
time, their relationship with the air,
their contempt for gravity,
that they are not of this earth.
They might be an alien species,
these interventions from above,
neither woman nor man,
and not quite animals, alas,
but rainbows made flesh,
an inspiration dressed in light.
Even as they turn their heads
to grant us an audience with the sun
we know they were created elsewhere
and will be going back there without us.

Deserters

Where did we think we were going,
two little suckers
setting off into the sunset
without a map or compass?
We travelled labyrinthine ways
to escape the forces of righteousness,
our map a blanket of stars.
We pulled it up to our chins.
Even now the search party is setting out
with torches and tracker dogs
to flush out the deserters.
Soon they will be waking us
from our dream-walk to nowhere,
dragging us back to our senses.

Dream-tatters

The saddest spring of venomous breezes,
our red-letter days torn off unused,
our plans on hold.
No walking out in rainbow weather,
no running home together.
Only hurrying strangers,
deserted pavements, enemy terrain.
The cheerful tears of cherry blossom flowers
fall round about, like the silk and satin
pink and white lace dream-tatters
that fell to our feet
and were happily kicked to one side
till this jealous second winter came
stalking between us.

The Letter

'Please don't be cross with me.
Nothing spectacular has happened
to make me hate you or anything.
I've just changed inside, that's all.
I suppose it was inevitable
that we couldn't go on like that,
but the feeling has been growing
since we last met, and now it's certain . . .'
The occasional awkward postcard
struggled back and forth between us,
which one day had to stop.
I would give her a call some time,
so we could arrange not to meet,
or talk about all that.

Hank Music

No credits roll across the sky
at the end of our story.
No tearful tracking shot
follows our wagon train
into Monument Valley.
Only 'Lovesick Blues'
mourns our passing.
Only 'Your Cheating Heart'
accompanies our slow fade
into clouds of our own dust.
The sky is dying under salt.
We join the hordes of extras
struggling over the horizon
as 'The End' comes into view.

Life at Sea

I ran outside to bum a cigarette
and found myself talking to a man
who knew what he was talking about.
He seemed to know you personally,
or someone very like you:
the same unreadable signals,
the same chains of yellow hair
lashing him to the mast in a storm.
He drew up the sides of his mouth
in a pleading, little girl face.
'Please sir, don't be cross with me.
I didn't mean for this to happen . . .'
He'd heard it all before, he said.
He likened it to seasickness.

Some Hope

Hope and Fear, those silly girls,
are the sound of a telephone ringing
on the other side of town,
begging her for mercy.
The little double cries
cling to the hem of her dress
as if they were drowning,
making her roll her eyes to heaven.
If it were up to me, of course,
I would never make such a call.
I would have more sense.
I would pull back from the brink
and hang up without saying anything,
knowing my number could be traced.

Night Starvation

I put three spoonfuls of Horlicks powder
in my least favourite mug,
pour on boiling milk
and give it a quick stir.
Everyone knows you aren't supposed
to boil the milk for Horlicks.
You have to make a paste first,
otherwise it doesn't mix.
I watch in sympathy
as the poor Horlicks bubbles
struggle to the surface of the mug
and burst open like spiders' eggs,
revealing interiors
full of dry Horlicks powder.

Night People

It is a darkened stage
where a single beam of light
flickers on silver paper costumes.
Regency bucks and belles
stiff-leg-it round the walls
in ghostly procession.
They jiggle and jerk for a moment
as if they were dancing.
Coming face to face with one another
in crudely outlined gardens,
they doff wide hats
and point little pointy shoes.
A little dog jumps up.
A butterfly waits in mid-air.

Sol y Sombra

I think of the luminous skeletons
hanging outside the old Sol y Sombra
where we used to dance.
They jiggled their bones in the wind,
bumping their bodies together
in the Latin American way.
London was our dancefloor then.
We danced our *danse macabre*
on the head of a pin.
We danced in the street afterwards,
suspended for a moment in time.
We bumped our bodies together
in the Latin American way.
We jiggled our bones in the wind.

Peace and Love

Through a gap in the curtains
I count the redundant chimney pots
on the houses opposite,
fifteen pot-bellied apostles,
preaching peace and love
to a sleeping world.
Someone has thrown a paper moon
onto a velvet ground
and added a handful of stars.
O night of fading fields
and children's sleep, become my will
which won't agree with me,
keep me busy counting chimney pots
while I seek an end to love.

Perfume or Light

Spurious desires after midnight,
the grey senior's irritable coughing,
his habitual re-telling of a story:
how she leant towards him once
in a shower of golden hair,
her waking infant stare,
her nunlike tears forming the links
of a chain still binding him.
Thoughts black as a stirred pool
dart hissing tongues, the self-inflicted shock
of understanding and dread
that love might be alive and well,
lying in wait for him some night
in a particular perfume or light.

Frosted Glass Weather

I was caught in the draught
between never going out and yet
never coming home: hesitant,
halfway places, landings and lifts,
where nobody lingers or loves,
or locked out of tall buildings
on hopeless football Saturdays,
lost for a light or a fight.
I was looking for a life
in frosted glass weather,
turning up my collar
at the corners of mean streets,
drawing back my lips
for the benefit of stray dogs.

Silver Tears

Which is why I break open the lines,
like breaking open a thermometer
and seeing the little silver tears
running around on the tabletop.
Line-breaks are time passing
in slow motion, mimicking our fate
with the terrible logic of gravity.
They step down into the street
or else they trip and fall
through cracks in our expectations.
I stand on a windy corner,
my head adrift in the dark currents
of the night. I taste on my tongue
the bitter truth of the stars.

Dateline

You were never so close
as when you were far away
in somewhere like New Zealand
or Japan. Great distances
like old-fashioned theatre make-up
heightened your cheekbones,
widened your stare across the Pacific.
Desire was some permanent tomorrow
hastening across datelines,
never quite arriving.
I only had to think of you
to find you gazing idly in my direction
with that calm, alert expression
of 'What on earth kept you?'

The Spare Room

We go back a long way, you and I,
on a mattress in the back of a van,
being thrown together
on the bumpy Welsh roads,
but having to wait
till we got to your parents' house
where we were supposed to be staying the night
before somebody's wedding.
You showed me into a freezing spare room
with a single iron bedstead,
'just to see the look on your face',
then burst out laughing.
We go back a long way, you and I.
I wish we could go there now.

Wilderness

The map we used
to find our way there
was mile for mile, air for air –
not so much the usual rough guide
to the rights and wrongs,
the ups and downs of life,
as the hazardous
enchanted wilderness
which lay between us.
I'm enclosing a copy of the thing
to remind you of the terrain
in case you feel inclined
to mark the spot with a cross
where we get back together again.

Slide Show

I watch them coming round
like scenes from someone's lecture on my life,
a carousel of hallucinations
left on by accident,
revolving endlessly in a darkened room:
the music, the night, and her,
perched on a late bar stool,
her hips and hair and shoulder blades
dawdling for a moment
in her body's slide show,
till the projector jams
and the apparition goes up in smoke,
a silent burn-hole blossoming
where her mouth used to be.

Blue Angel

With what tender brave wounds
her version of 'Blue Angel'
sheds forgiving tears.
The piano's rippling sobs
obey each helpless phrase
as if they were my own.
'Don't you worry, pretty dear,
I'll never let you down, Blue Angel . . .'
If I could conjure her face
out of this cry for lost love,
I would carry her back to a place
where broken songs are mended.
I would pay good tears
to hear Blue Angel sing.

The Story So Far

At this point in the story
all we can say for sure
is that one of us goes on ahead
to explore the difficult terrain
where everything remains to be seen,
while the other stays home,
tossed this way and that
on the cross-currents of memory.
There's no such thing as a plot.
We climb up into the fork
of the tallest tree
and kick the ladder away.
We can see clearly from here,
but we may need some help with the ending.